Lancashire Poets

Edited By Kyra Eyles

Years of YoungWriters

First published in Great Britain in 2017 by:

Young Writers
Remus House
Coltsfoot Drive
Peterborough
PE2 9BF
Telephone: 01733 890066
Website: www.youngwriters.co.uk

SB ISBN 978-1-78820-396-8
Printed and bound in the UK by BookPrintingUK
Website: www.bookprintinguk.com
YB0333G

Foreword

Dear Reader,

Welcome to this book packed full of feathery, furry and scaly friends!

Young Writers' Poetry Safari competition was specifically designed for 5-7 year-olds as a fun introduction to poetry and as a way to think about the world of animals. They could write about pets, exotic animals, dinosaurs and you'll even find a few crazy creatures that have never been seen before! From this starting point, the poems could be as simple or as elaborate as the writer wanted, using imagination and descriptive language.

Given the young age of the entrants, we have tried to include as many poems as possible. Here at Young Writers we believe that seeing their work in print will inspire a love of reading and writing and give these young poets the confidence to develop their skills in the future. Poetry is a wonderful way to introduce young children to the idea of rhyme and rhythm and helps learning and development of communication, language and literacy skills.

These young poets have used their creative writing abilities, sentence structure skills, thoughtful vocabulary and most importantly, their imaginations, to make their poems and the animals within them come alive. I hope you enjoy reading them as much as we have.

Kyra Eyles

Contents

Cedars Primary School, Blackburn

Adam Hameed (6), Areeba Ali, Amna, Tauhid Bapu, Zahraa Jan & Sumayah	1
Eshal Ahmad (7), Hamzah Munaf Umerji, Faiz, Sadeem & Tasneem	2
Aneesha Khan (6), Shahzaib Butt (5), Umar Patel, Aimun Malik, Hadia-Batool, Yahya, Kowiar, Aliza Perwez (6) & Salwa Shahid	3
Hiba Hussain (6) & Tehreem Hussain (6)	4
Jagjeevan Maan Singh (6)	5
Zara Javid Dhoriwala (6), Narmeen Khan, Muhammed Hashim & Fayez	6
Laaibah Nazir (6), Manoor Raza (7), Laylah, Subhan, Fatima, Faheem Hussain (6) & Amina Tufail (6)	7
Awais Younas (6), Ayaan, Hanzalah Chopdat, Neha Wasim, Ameerah Haque & Reyhana	8
Ethan Fleming (6)	9
Irfan Alom (6)	10

Christ Church Ainsworth CE Primary School, Bolton

Austin Liam Townsend (6)	11
Kendal Reanie Parkinson Gowing (7)	12
Freya Franklin (7)	13
Thomas Leece (7)	14

Lily-Mae Newton (7)	15
Lilly-Grace Commins (7)	16
Hollie Mai Simms (7)	17
Annabelle Grace Unsworth (7)	18
Gracie Robertson-Burns (7)	19
Eloise Russell-Gray (6)	20
Bella Walton (6)	21
Dylan Johnston-Timperley (6)	22
Ronan Sheikh (6)	23
Oliver Harry Scott (7)	24
Lucy Tracey (7)	25
Charlotte Erin Lees (7)	26
Princess Cartwright (7)	27
Oliver Horrocks (7)	28
Jessica Rose Carroll (7)	29
Jacob Ewan Farnworth (6)	30
Rory Freestone (7)	31
Katie Baines (7)	32
Harry Jenkinson (7)	33
Adin Knowles (7)	34

Clarendon Cottage Prep School, Eccles

Emmie Hartley (6)	35
Adam Yunis (6)	36
Lucy Grace Campbell (5)	37
Enzo Hoffe (5)	38
Isabelle Hulme (6)	39
Arthur Andrews (6)	40
William Robert Kelly (6)	41

Fulwood St Peter's CE Primary School, Fulwood

Oliver Coupland (7)	42
Natalia Ntai (6)	43
Freya Newson-Nixon (7)	44
Zack Young (7)	45
Solomon Evans (6)	46
Benjamin Hallmark (7)	47
Owais Musa (7)	48
Anna Ibin-Ibrahim (6)	49
Charlotte Claire Bowdidge (7)	50
Raeef Tanveer (7)	51
Lila Newson-Nixon (7)	52
Nathaniel Collie (7)	53
Rachel Reuben (6)	54
Nishka Singh (7)	55
Lucia Thorp (6)	56
Lucy Lai (7)	57
Miles Laurence Williamson (6)	58
Grace Lochhead (7)	59
Alex Hodson (6)	60
Fazil Darwan (6)	61
Mahira Ulfat Mannan (7)	62
Jonathan William Holderness (6)	63
Stanley Fred Jones (7)	64

Greenbank Primary School, Rochdale

Hasaan Ahmed (6)	65
Tyler Tyson Wormald (7)	66
Inaaya Inny Iram (7)	67
Noreen Ahmmed (7)	68
Khadija Akhtar (7)	69
Malaikah Insar (7)	70
Abrar Ahmed Abadi (7)	71
Parishe Anjam (6)	72
Mohammed Saif Waseem (6)	73
Iman Khan (6)	74
Jemima Khan (7)	75
Benjamin Marinelli-Fletcher (7)	76
Alam A (7)	77
Rachael Olawale (7)	78

Danish Shoukat (7)	79

Haslingden Primary School, Haslingden

Jumainah Bibi (7)	80
Tiffany Dunn (7)	81
Ana-Maria Khanom (7)	82
Beck Harrison (7)	83
Harvey Allan (7)	84
Farrah Slman (7)	85
Annie Devlin (7)	86
Abbie Cokell (6)	87
Joshua Prater (7)	88
Maheen Yousuf (7)	89
Jamal Khan (7)	90
Tanisha Hasan (7)	91
Findlay George Curness (6)	92
Mohammed Mohsin Iqbal (7)	93
Amelia Hobson (7)	94
Afreen Ali (7)	95
Areeb Aamir (13)	96
Dhaniyaal Khan (7)	97

Pool House Community Primary School, Ingol

Darcy Morrison (6)	98
Alicja Wojtkielewicz (6)	99
Arham Ali (6)	100
Esther Uchechukwu Imoh (6)	101
Philip Michalkowski (6)	102
Lily-May Cookson (5)	103
Caroline Duncan (6)	104
Alan Kacprowicz (6)	105
Kayden Lee Scott (6)	106
Kacey May Pickup (6)	107

The Poems

Tigers Senses Poem

The tigers look like stripy angry bees.
The tigers feel fluffy, soft
and smooth like a blanket.
The tigers look like a loud washing machine.
The tigers taste like meaty pasta
and boiled eggs.
The tigers smell like kitchen cleaning spray
and rotten fish.

Adam Hameed (6), Areeba Ali, Amna, Tauhid Bapu, Zahraa Jan & Sumayah
Cedars Primary School, Blackburn

Penguin Senses Poem

Penguins taste like freezing chocolate
And vanilla ice cream.
Penguins are white and black
And really wet.
They waddle when they move.
They make happy lovely seal sounds.
Penguins feel soft and cuddly like a pillow.
They smell like sweet fish.

Eshal Ahmad (7), Hamzah Munaf Umerji, Faiz, Sadeem & Tasneem
Cedars Primary School, Blackburn

Polar Bear Senses Poem

Polar bears look as white as a cloud.
Polar bears smell like fresh fish cooked
in the oven.
Polar bears sound like an angry T-rex.
Polar bears are cuddly
like my big teddy bear.
Polar bears taste like mashed potato
and marshmallows.

Aneesha Khan (6), Shahzaib Butt (5), Umar Patel, Aimun Malik, Hadia-Batool, Yahya, Kowiar, Aliza Perwez (6) & Salwa Shahid
Cedars Primary School, Blackburn

Jaguar Senses Poem

A jaguar is spotty and it is a big cat.
A jaguar sounds like a roaring dinosaur.
A jaguar smells like a fresh fish.
A jaguar feels like a soft fluffy pillow.
A jaguar tastes like a rotten fish.

Hiba Hussain (6) & Tehreem Hussain (6)

Cedars Primary School, Blackburn

Snow Leopard Senses Poem

The snow leopard looks like a huge white cloud.
The snow leopard shouts like a tiger.
The snow leopard smells like stinky fish.
The snow leopard feels like a soft pillow.
The snow leopard tastes like stinky fish.

Jagjeevan Maan Singh (6)
Cedars Primary School, Blackburn

Giraffe Senses Poem

Giraffes smell like grass and hay.
Giraffes look like tall trees
And have a spotty body.
Giraffes feel smooth and warm.
Giraffes taste like chocolate and banana.
Giraffes make crunchy and munchy sounds.

Zara Javid Dhoriwala (6), Narmeen Khan, Muhammed Hashim & Fayez
Cedars Primary School, Blackburn

Peacocks Senses Poem

Peacocks look colourful
And sparkly like glitter.
Peacocks smell like mints.
Peacocks feel smooth and cool like a fan.
Peacocks taste of blue, sticky bubblegum.
Peacocks are loud and confident.

Laaibah Nazir (6), Manoor Raza (7), Laylah, Subhan, Fatima, Faheem Hussain (6) & Amina Tufail (6)
Cedars Primary School, Blackburn

Monkey Senses Poem

Monkeys look brown like a chocolate bar.
Monkeys sound loud and scream *ooo, aaaa*.
Monkeys smell like yummy bananas.
Monkeys feel soft and cuddly.
Monkeys taste fluffy like candyfloss.

Awais Younas (6), Ayaan, Hanzalah Chopdat, Neha Wasim, Ameerah Haque & Reyhana
Cedars Primary School, Blackburn

Giraffe Senses Poem

A giraffe looks like a long-necked lion.
A giraffe sounds like crunching leaves
when eating.
A giraffe smells like bananas.
A giraffe feels like a puppy.
A giraffe tastes like a lemon.

Ethan Fleming (6)
Cedars Primary School, Blackburn

Snow Leopard Senses Poem

The snow leopard looks like white soft snow.
The snow leopard roars like a dragon.
The snow leopard smells like rotten meat.
The snow leopard feels like a comfy pillow.

Irfan Alom (6)
Cedars Primary School, Blackburn

Mythical Monster

It's as mysterious as a bat with no wings.
It's as dusty as a python.
It erases minds like a machine.
It's as dark as a shadow.
Its one thousand fangs are like screwdrivers
And as scary as a dragon.
It's as bloodthirsty as a vampire.
It's the mythical creature, Mysterio!

Austin Liam Townsend (6)

Christ Church Ainsworth CE Primary School, Bolton

The Dolphin Show

She is as glamorous as the Queen
But she only eats fish.
She lives in the sea.
She is as reliable as Mr Matheson.
She is as blue as the sky.
She'll let me ride on her back.
She jumps in the air.
She is as cute as a polar bear.
She's my dolphin friend who lives in the sea.

Kendal Reanie Parkinson Gowing (7)
Christ Church Ainsworth CE Primary School, Bolton

Guess Who I Am?

She is as fat as a pig.
She is as cute as a puppy.
She is smellier than sewage.
She is black and white like a cat.
She eats bamboo.
She is as weird as a monkey.
She is as slow as a snail.
She is furrier than a horse.
She is as greedy as my brother.
She is a panda.

Freya Franklin (7)

Christ Church Ainsworth CE Primary School, Bolton

What Am I?

It is skinny like an elephant.
It is long like a tree.
It is smooth like a pillow.
It is spotty like a Dalmatian.
It is brown like a bear.
It is slithery like a snake.
It is as white as snow.
It is black like a gorilla.
It is a python.

Thomas Leece (7)
Christ Church Ainsworth CE Primary School, Bolton

Queen Giraffe

She is as elegant as a bird.
She is as tall as a giant.
Her neck is as long as a tree trunk.
She has long eyelashes like a beautiful girl.
She is an elegant walker like a ballerina.
She is as important as a queen.
She is my giraffe.

Lily-Mae Newton (7)
Christ Church Ainsworth CE Primary School, Bolton

What's My Animal?

It is as fast as a wave.
It as yellow as the desert.
It is as greedy as a monkey.
It is as spotty as a giraffe.
It is as long as a snake when it leaps.
As terrific as a kangaroo.
It is as nasty as a lion.
It is a cheetah!

Lilly-Grace Commins (7)
Christ Church Ainsworth CE Primary School, Bolton

My Animal

He is as graceful as a giraffe.
He is as naughty as a schoolboy.
He is as fast as my teacher.
His tail is as squishy as an elephant's.
He clip-clops like a unicorn.
He is as greedy as a pig.
He bucks like a crazy horse.

Hollie Mai Simms (7)

Christ Church Ainsworth CE Primary School, Bolton

I Am Fast

It is as fast as a car on the motorway.
It hates water like a cat.
It is as spotty as a leopard.
It hunts like a lion.
It is as black and spotty as a rug.
It is as gingery yellow as a dandy lion.
It's a cheetah.

Annabelle Grace Unsworth (7)
Christ Church Ainsworth CE Primary School, Bolton

Remarkable Swan

She is as remarkable as a star.
She is as magnificent as a princess.
She is as elegant as a cat.
She is as calm as a baby.
She is as white as blossom.
She shimmers like gold.
She is as beautiful as a flamingo.

Gracie Robertson-Burns (7)

Christ Church Ainsworth CE Primary School, Bolton

What Am I?

It's as fluffy as a kitten.
It's as spotty as a domino.
It's as slow as a snail.
It's as cute as a newborn baby.
It's as happy as my teacher.
It's as greedy as a pig.
It's my dog, Yogi!

Eloise Russell-Gray (6)
Christ Church Ainsworth CE Primary School, Bolton

The Glamorous Unicorn

She is as wild as a bear.

She is as friendly as Mr Heaton.

She is as mysterious as a haunted house.

She is as beautiful as a rose.

She is a herbivore like a dinosaur.

She is as magical as a star.

She is a unicorn.

Bella Walton (6)

Christ Church Ainsworth CE Primary School, Bolton

What Am I?

He is as dangerous as a dragon.
As violent as a soldier
And is as deadly as a viper
And he eats squirrels, dogs and snakes.
He has razor-sharp claws
And 75,000 teeth
And strong wings.
He is a hippogryph.

Dylan Johnston-Timperley (6)
Christ Church Ainsworth CE Primary School, Bolton

The Cheetah King

It is as fast as Usain Bolt.
It is as strong as a bear
And as big as a tiger.
It is as spotty as a leopard
And as yellow as the sun.
Its tail is as long as a giraffe's.
It's a cheetah!

Ronan Sheikh (6)
Christ Church Ainsworth CE Primary School, Bolton

This Is Me

I am as massive as a tree.
I am elegant like a swan.
I am as spotty as a Dalmatian.
I am as thin as a cardboard box.
I am as black as a spider.
I am as yellow as the sun.
It's me, a giraffe!

Oliver Harry Scott (7)

Christ Church Ainsworth CE Primary School, Bolton

What Am I?

She is as cute as an owl.
She is as brown as a bear.
She is as loving as a giraffe.
She is a sun diamond.
She is as skinny as a robin's legs.
She is as brown as a horse
And as caring as me.

Lucy Tracey (7)
Christ Church Ainsworth CE Primary School, Bolton

Monkey Story

It is loud like a lion.
It is as silly as a clown.
It eats bananas all the time
Because it loves them.
It has beautiful brown skin like a bull.
It lives in trees.
It is as glorious as a bird.

Charlotte Erin Lees (7)
Christ Church Ainsworth CE Primary School, Bolton

Untitled

It can jump like a kangaroo
And is as lovely as a flamingo.
It has a tail as long as a snake
And is as clever as my teacher.
It can spin round like a wheel
And has ears as black as an ant.

Princess Cartwright (7)

Christ Church Ainsworth CE Primary School, Bolton

The Lion King

It is as strong as a tiger.
It has yellow skin like a lemon.
It has a big head like a tiger.
It is as hairy as a cheetah.
It has a long tail like a monkey.
It has blue eyes like the ocean.

Oliver Horrocks (7)
Christ Church Ainsworth CE Primary School, Bolton

The Furious Cheetah

She is as fit as John Cena.
She is as quiet as a mouse.
She is as furious and fast as Usain Bolt.
She is as strong as Mr Matheson.
She is as elegant as a giraffe.
She is Lola the cheetah.

Jessica Rose Carroll (7)

Christ Church Ainsworth CE Primary School, Bolton

Small And Brown...

It is as cute as a puppy.
It is as fast as Mo Farah.
It is as small as a pig.
It is as brown as a bear.
It has fur as smooth as silk.
It is as cuddly as a teddy.
It is a guinea pig.

Jacob Ewan Farnworth (6)
Christ Church Ainsworth CE Primary School, Bolton

Black

She is as cute as a cake.

She is as small as a rabbit.

She is as fascinating as a dinosaur.

She is as jumpy as a kangaroo.

She is black and white like a zebra.

She is my pet cat, Moggy.

Rory Freestone (7)

Christ Church Ainsworth CE Primary School, Bolton

It's Me

He is as cheeky as my teacher.
He is as funny as my brother.
He is as greedy as a dog.
He loves bananas just like me.
He can swing like a circus performer.
He is as naughty as a bear.

Katie Baines (7)

Christ Church Ainsworth CE Primary School, Bolton

The Prickly Hedgehog

It kills slugs and snails like a frog.
It is as greedy as my dad.
It scuffles like thunder.
It is as spiky and prickly as the gruffalo.
It is as quiet as a mouse.

Harry Jenkinson (7)
Christ Church Ainsworth CE Primary School, Bolton

What Animal Is It?

It is as spotty as a dice.
It is as yellow as a daffodil.
It is faster than Harry.
It is as hairy as a dog.
It is as creepy as a snake.
It is as big as a giant.

Adin Knowles (7)
Christ Church Ainsworth CE Primary School, Bolton

The Outstanding Turtle

As the turtle swims
she smells like salted rock.
The turtle looks outstanding
as she carries her shell with pride.
The turtle feels very lumpy, rock solid
and also very slimy.
The turtle sounds like it's hissing
and squealing.
The turtle tastes like a crunchy
and slimy snail.

Emmie Hartley (6)
Clarendon Cottage Prep School, Eccles

Dangerous Manta Ray

As the manta ray flaps his wings
Be careful of his tail.
Squishy and harsh without fail.
The manta ray tastes like rubbery skin,
Not like a rubbery fin.
The manta ray sounds medium squishy
As it flaps around the sea.

Adam Yunis (6)
Clarendon Cottage Prep School, Eccles

The Fabulous Seahorse

In the ocean the seahorse looks very proud,
like my mum.
She sounds squeaky, like an amazing
dolphin.
She tastes like a splendid fish.
She feels like a soft, smooth rubber.
She smells of salty water from the sea.

Lucy Grace Campbell (5)
Clarendon Cottage Prep School, Eccles

Sneaky Swordfish

Looks sneaky and very shiny.
Smells of rotten fish.
Feels smooth on his back
but sharp on his sword.
Sounds like a knight's sword running
into battle.
Tastes like a manta ray inside out.

Enzo Hoffe (5)
Clarendon Cottage Prep School, Eccles

The Amazing Pufferfish

It feels like a bumpy snake.
It tastes like a duck from a book.
It smells, I can't tell,
I think it smells like shells.
Looks like a curled-up snake.
Sounds the same as the birds.

Isabelle Hulme (6)
Clarendon Cottage Prep School, Eccles

The Speedy Swordfish

The speedy swordfish is really shiny.
The speedy swordfish tastes
like a human stuck on a sunken ship.
It feels really smooth with a sharp,
pointy nose.
It smells of salty chocolate.

Arthur Andrews (6)
Clarendon Cottage Prep School, Eccles

The Ugly Shark

You can hear the shark swishing
It looks like a swordfish
But without a sword on its head.
It tastes like an ugly fish.
It smells like it is seawater.

William Robert Kelly (6)
Clarendon Cottage Prep School, Eccles

The Busy Safari

I can hear the cheeky cheetahs chewing
on the meat.
I can see the golden lions basking
in the heat.
I can smell the different creatures stomping
to and fro.
I can taste the dusty breeze blowing up
my nose.
I can hear the elephants squirting water
from their trunks.
I can see the mud covered hippos,
I think they must have sunk.
I can smell the juicy meat being followed
by a cheetah to eat.
I can taste the dirty mud being flicked
into my mouth.
What a busy safari.

Oliver Coupland (7)
Fulwood St Peter's CE Primary School, Fulwood

Safari Poems

I can taste the dust as dusty as soft sand.
I can feel the leopard's fur as smooth
as my freshly washed hand.
I can see the cheeky cheetahs sprinting
as fast as a race car.
I can smell the old meat as ancient
as an old grandma.

I can hear a loud leopard eating
under the bright stars.
I can see the leopard leaping
near and far.
I can hear the loud leopard
growling for its meat.
I can smell the smelly breath
as smelly as my feet!

Natalia Ntai (6)
Fulwood St Peter's CE Primary School, Fulwood

Busy Safari

I can hear the elephant trumpeting,
hyena laughing, crocodile snapping.
I can see the cheetahs racing their prey
as fast as lightning.
Quick, quick, quick, run, run, run
or it'll eat your tum.
Pitter-patter, pitter-patter raindrops
in the heat.
The animals are enjoying all the juicy meat.
I can see the hyena hiding from the rain.
I can see the elephants rolling in the dirt
down the lane.

Freya Newson-Nixon (7)
Fulwood St Peter's CE Primary School, Fulwood

The Cheeky Cheetahs

I can see the cheetahs sucking
the shiny water.
I can hear the cheeky cheetahs roaring
at other animals.
I can smell the cheeky cheetahs
eating their dinner
and they will have smelly breath.
I can see the cheeky cheetahs
chasing other animals.
I can feel the cheeky cheetah's soft fur.
I can taste the gritty sand
blowing in my mouth.

Zack Young (7)
Fulwood St Peter's CE Primary School, Fulwood

Africa

See the lions on the prowl.
Big, furry mane and a fearsome growl.
Colours of orange, brown and red,
Sun beaming down upon the dusty bed.

I can taste the dusty feet of the lion
As dusty as a construction site.
Beautiful sunset melting down
On the space of the ground.
All is quiet and calm,
Now the stars come down
And light the way.

Solomon Evans (6)
Fulwood St Peter's CE Primary School, Fulwood

Elephant Poem

I can hear the loud elephants throwing
their lovely trunks in the flower breeze,
out squirts water, beware!
I can hear the stomping feet as
loud as a loud dinosaur.
I can hear them nursing their babies,
licking their soft paws.
I can hear the elephants squelching
in the dirty mud.
I can hear them rolling around
looking with a thud.

Benjamin Hallmark (7)
Fulwood St Peter's CE Primary School, Fulwood

All About Safari

I saw a cheetah
Long and fierce,
Yellow and black,
Faster than a Lamborghini,
Faster than Usain Bolt!

Look, spot, sprint, attack,
This is how a cheetah lives.
I can hear a cheetah,
Loud and rough,
Hungry and impatient.

Greedier than a wolf,
Look, spot, sprint, attack
This is how a cheetah lives.

Owais Musa (7)
Fulwood St Peter's CE Primary School, Fulwood

The Safari

I can see play fighting cheetahs
in the distance.
I can hear the grumpy growls as
loud as a truck.
I can feel the stinky sand as rough
as sandpaper.
I can smell the minty meat
as minty as toothpaste.
I can taste the horrible, hot sweat
as smelly as a pigsty.
There are lots of things to see, smell
and hear on a safari.

Anna Ibin-Ibrahim (6)

Fulwood St Peter's CE Primary School, Fulwood

Leaping Leopards

I can see the leaping leopards
jumping to and fro.
I can taste the horrible sand
like play dough.
I can smell the lovely leopards
as lovely as a rose.
I can feel the soft, smooth sand
as soft as a leopard's fur coat.
I can hear scraping paws of a leopard
jumping far and near.
I love the safari!
There is no fear!

Charlotte Claire Bowdidge (7)
Fulwood St Peter's CE Primary School, Fulwood

A Busy Safari

I can hear the lion roaring on the safari
and looking at me, running as fast as a car.
I can see the lion stomping fast,
louder than a dinosaur.
I can feel the thin and furry skin
as soft as a blanket.
I can taste the disgusting dust
at a muddy puddle.
I can smell the delicious meat
ready for the lion's dinner.

Raeef Tanveer (7)
Fulwood St Peter's CE Primary School, Fulwood

All About Safari

Hot, hot, hot, sun, sun, sun
makes the animals slump, slump, slump.
Listen now, you can hear the cheetahs
running in fear.
Look out gazelle, behind you
a hungry cheetah is after you.
Watch out, don't let the crocodiles
in the river jump out.
Smell the stinky meat rotting away
in the boiling heat.

Lila Newson-Nixon (7)
Fulwood St Peter's CE Primary School, Fulwood

Safari Is Fun

Golden hair surrounds my face,
I run and leap from rock to rock,
Place to place.
Prey I see, it is a goat
With a beautiful shiny coat.
Time for tea,
I run behind a tree.
I leap and bounce
And I pounce.
Food at last,
I gobble it fast.
The wind ruffles my fur,
I give a contented purr.

Nathaniel Collie (7)
Fulwood St Peter's CE Primary School, Fulwood

The Busy Safari

I can feel a soft hippo as soft as a pancake.
I can taste a crunchy apple as crunchy
as a paper.
I can see a roaring lion calling his friends.
I can smell the dust from a lion's paw.
I can hear the lion stamping as loud
as a hippo's feet.
The safari is a really busy place to be!

Rachel Reuben (6)

Fulwood St Peter's CE Primary School, Fulwood

A Cheetah Poem

I can hear cheeky cheetahs laughing
as they play.
I can see the cheeky cheetahs
sprinting far away.
I can feel the cheeky cheetah's
soft and furry coat.
I can taste the juicy meat,
maybe it's a goat.
I can smell the stinky sand
as smelly as a pig.
Wow! This safari is so big!

Nishka Singh (7)
Fulwood St Peter's CE Primary School, Fulwood

The Busy Safari

I can see the leopards running
as fast as a car.
I can see the monkeys in the Jeep
as cheeky as a clown.
I can see the elephants rolling in the mud
as happy as a child.
I can see the giraffes munching leaves
from the skyscraper trees.
I can see lots of great animals on a safari.

Lucia Thorp (6)
Fulwood St Peter's CE Primary School, Fulwood

All About A Safari

I can taste the smelly hooves
walking the ground.
I can hear the loud tiger making
lots of sounds.
I can see the hungry tigers
eating the juicy meat.
I can smell the stinky sand
underneath my feet!
There are lots of things to smell and see
when you go on a safari.

Lucy Lai (7)
Fulwood St Peter's CE Primary School, Fulwood

The Busy Safari

I can hear loud stomping as loud
as a building site.
I can taste the delicious bark
as delicious as tasty fruit.
I can smell a stinky elephant
as stinky as seaweed.
I can feel the soft sand sticking to my feet.
I can see the burning sun as hot as Mars.

Miles Laurence Williamson (6)
Fulwood St Peter's CE Primary School, Fulwood

Leaping Leopards

I can see leaping leopards running very fast.
I can see tall giraffes as tall as a skyscraper.
I can see camouflaged leopards
keeping undercover.
I can see the leaping leopards hopping
rock to rock.
I can see the huge hippos as huge
as a boulder.

Grace Lochhead (7)
Fulwood St Peter's CE Primary School, Fulwood

African Animals

I can hear lions as loud as thunder.
The sun beaming upon the lion's skin
as golden as a snake.
Out squirts water, beware!
Big shiny mane and a fearsome growl.
Tasting the dust of the elephant's foot.
The safari is a wonderful place to be.

Alex Hodson (6)
Fulwood St Peter's CE Primary School, Fulwood

I Love The Safari

I can taste the tasty meat.
I can feel sand coming under my feet.
I can hear the beats coming
from the lion's feet.
I can see the other animals from my sleep.
I can smell the stinky sand in the warm
and dusty heat.

Fazil Darwan (6)
Fulwood St Peter's CE Primary School, Fulwood

Untitled

I can see a muddy pool as dirty as a pig.
I can hear the elephants splashing
in the mud.
I can smell the fresh leaves ready for dinner.
I can taste the cold fresh water flowing.
I can feel the sand underneath my feet.

Mahira Ulfat Mannan (7)
Fulwood St Peter's CE Primary School, Fulwood

The Safari

I can see the elephants stomping
on the hard ground.
I can smell the fresh meat ready
for the tigers.
I can hear the giraffe chomping
the fresh meat.
I can taste the dirty sand blowing
in my mouth.

Jonathan William Holderness (6)
Fulwood St Peter's CE Primary School, Fulwood

The Safari

I can see soft sand.
I can hear the stomping steps.
I can smell the dirty dust.
I can feel the soft fur.
I can taste the sand in my mouth.

Stanley Fred Jones (7)
Fulwood St Peter's CE Primary School, Fulwood

Something Spotty

Fish chaser
Colour splasher
Meat eater
Shrimp eater
Fast swimmer
Scary gnashers
Quick eater
Ocean fighter
Hurting stinger
Seaworms hunter
Strong fighter
Ocean swimmer
Good hunter.

Hasaan Ahmed (6)
Greenbank Primary School, Rochdale

Guess The Sea Creature

Blue and white
Eats people, fish and seals
Lives in deep water
Different temperatures
Sharp teeth
Spiky pectoral fin
Mammals
Eats sea lions
Baby whales
Eats meat
Eats squid.

Tyler Tyson Wormald (7)

Greenbank Primary School, Rochdale

Something Sneaky

Squid eater
Fish eater
Sneaky hider
Underground muncher
Fast eater
Speedy traveller
Creepy follower
Sneaky eater
Scary muncher
Scary creature
Black creature.

Inaaya Inny Iram (7)
Greenbank Primary School, Rochdale

Something Electric

Meat shredder
Electric shocker
Human eater
Fast slither
Sly shocker
Scary eater
Fearsome hunter
Sly hider
Bone shocker
Fierce killer
Sharp eater.

Noreen Ahmmed (7)

Greenbank Primary School, Rochdale

Eel

Fish eater
Fast swimmer
Sneaky prowler
Big smiler
Hungry eater
Sneaky finder
Human killer
Scary chaser
Bone breaker
Good hider
Shiny shopper.

Khadija Akhtar (7)
Greenbank Primary School, Rochdale

A Poem About A Clownfish

Algae eater
Sea creature
Orange eater
Little swimmer
Cute smiler
Hungry eater
Fast swimmer
Stripy smiler
Small creature
Orange creature.

Malaikah Insar (7)
Greenbank Primary School, Rochdale

Something Watery

A splashy player
A fantastic swimmer
A shrimp eater
A good diver
A smooth feeler
A happy smiler
A friendly diver
An exciting watcher.

Abrar Ahmed Abadi (7)
Greenbank Primary School, Rochdale

Something Playful

A splashy player
A happy swimmer
An excited jumper
A great diver
A silly slipper
A happy smiler
A friendly eater
An entertaining player.

Parishe Anjam (6)
Greenbank Primary School, Rochdale

Stingray

Long, spotty
Pointy tail
Pointy stingray
Long creature
Pointy tail
Stingy spine
Sharp spine
Big eyes
Greedy eater
Meat eater.

Mohammed Saif Waseem (6)

Greenbank Primary School, Rochdale

Big Shark

It swims speedily
and it never stops swimming.
It likes everything.
It likes fish a lot
and it is not afraid of anything,
it is brave.

Iman Khan (6)
Greenbank Primary School, Rochdale

Silent Starfish

Slow swimmer
Hungry eater
Spiky scales
Colourful creature
Ocean swimmer
Cute player
Sticky sticker.

Jemima Khan (7)
Greenbank Primary School, Rochdale

Guess Who?

House carrier
Meat eater
Egg layer
Tropical liver
Oval swimmer
Strong swimmer
Good diver.

Benjamin Marinelli-Fletcher (7)
Greenbank Primary School, Rochdale

Seahorses

Colourful and curly.
Curly and whirly.
Cold creature.
Long creature.

Alam A (7)

Greenbank Primary School, Rochdale

Seahorses

A soft creature.
A fast swimmer.
A good runner.
A scary eater.

Rachael Olawale (7)
Greenbank Primary School, Rochdale

Something Wobbly

Fish eater
Special stinger
Wiggly swimmer.

Danish Shoukat (7)

Greenbank Primary School, Rochdale

Pirate's Parrot

The parrot is blue, red and yellow.
It has orange wings and a peach face.
It also has a purple, brown
And dark purple hat.
It likes flying and playing.
It also likes playing teachers.
It listens to the pirate
And copies the pirate.
It doesn't like staying in its cage
And it doesn't like eating.
It also likes going on adventures
Or journeys with the pirate.
The pirate hates it.
It never sleeps.
It eats seeds and nuts.

Jumainah Bibi (7)
Haslingden Primary School, Haslingden

A Pirate's Pet Cheetah

C lever, naughty cheetah loves to run fast
H appy little cheetah loves to pounce
E very little disaster she can solve
E ach time she chases off the rats she
  throws them off the ship
T oday she runs as fast as she can
A naughty little cheetah, run, run, run
H orrible cheetah runs but please slow
  down.

Tiffany Dunn (7)
Haslingden Primary School, Haslingden

Tiana's Trusty Parrot Tiki

Tiana's parrot is so sweet,
It listens to every instruction.
She makes sure everyone is okay
and safe.
My parrot likes to look for shiny gold
and silver treasure.
When they find treasure they share it
with everyone else on the island.

Ana-Maria Khanom (7)
Haslingden Primary School, Haslingden

A Pirate's Pet

T reacherous turtle taps you on the back
U nder the sea turtle is fine
R unning with a ruler turtle finds it hard
T oo many pirates give him jobs
L eopards he is afraid of
E verybody knows he is a pirate.

Beck Harrison (7)

Haslingden Primary School, Haslingden

A Pirate's Pet Shark

S hips are wrecked with big shiny fangs

H e swims eating every fish that he passes

A pirate can't beat this shark, it is too strong

R ight thing to do is abandon ship

K illing is not a peaceful sound.

Harvey Allan (7)

Haslingden Primary School, Haslingden

The Pirate's Parrot

The parrot is beautiful.
What is the parrot like?
What do the parrots eat?
What do the parrots like to do?
Your parrot is nice.
Your parrot is furry.
What does your parrot like to eat?
Does your parrot talk?

Farrah Slman (7)
Haslingden Primary School, Haslingden

My Parrot Poem

My parrot likes to fly in the sky
And says, 'Get out of the way,'
And soars through the sky
And copies the crew
And says, 'Ahoy me hearties.'
And sleeps on his head
And says, 'Get up.'

Annie Devlin (7)
Haslingden Primary School, Haslingden

Pirate's Pet Monkey

M y cheeky monkey
O ld monkey sits down
N ever pinch a banana
K eep a monkey in the right place
E at the right food monkey
Y ou are brown.

Abbie Cokell (6)
Haslingden Primary School, Haslingden

A Pirate's Pet Spider

S pider eats flies

P erches on bugs

I n a sticky web made of silk

D on't rip his web

E very time he is hungry

R olls away from danger.

Joshua Prater (7)
Haslingden Primary School, Haslingden

A Pirate's Pet Pony

H orse likes to eat anything apart from squid
O nly if you give her chips with it
R oll in the ship
S he is often happy
E very day she has fun.

Maheen Yousuf (7)
Haslingden Primary School, Haslingden

A Pirate's Pet Snake

S lithery snake always moves
N avigates his location
A re in the ships
K erinya pirate is a kind pirate
E verybody is a pirate.

Jamal Khan (7)

Haslingden Primary School, Haslingden

My Parrot

My parrot is called Tom.
Tom has a fierce face.
He has a captain who is his friend.
He blows fire because no one is about
To steal money from the captain.

Tanisha Hasan (7)

Haslingden Primary School, Haslingden

Captain Blimp The Parrot

Captain Blimp is courageous.
Captain Blimp is brave and pecky.
Captain Blimp's pirate owners
are kind to him.
Captain Blimp is intelligent.

Findlay George Curness (6)
Haslingden Primary School, Haslingden

Parrot

Parrot, parrot
Sit on my shoulder.
Parrot, look at me.
Parrot, parrot
Sit on my shoulder
Or sit in the ship maybe.
Fly now parrot!

Mohammed Mohsin Iqbal (7)
Haslingden Primary School, Haslingden

Bright Parrot

Once upon a time
There was a parrot
On a pirate's shoulder.
It was gold and red.
This parrot had an enormous tail.

Amelia Hobson (7)

Haslingden Primary School, Haslingden

About A Parrot

This parrot is colourful.
He sings a song lovely
And it sounds great.
He eats mushy fish.
He makes sounds.

Afreen Ali (7)
Haslingden Primary School, Haslingden

The Pirate's Parrot

My parrot stands on my hand
At home and at Brayford.
My parrot does magic tricks.
My parrot is called Mango.

Areeb Aamir (13)
Haslingden Primary School, Haslingden

The Intelligent Parrot

My parrot is intelligent,
Beautiful, colourful,
Fast, clever,
Smart and red.
He has a white beak.

Dhaniyaal Khan (7)

Haslingden Primary School, Haslingden

If I Were...

If I were a flamingo
I would have pink feathers
And be pretty.
If I were a flamingo
I would stand on one leg and make sounds,
But for now, I'm happy to be me.

Darcy Morrison (6)
Pool House Community Primary School, Ingol

If I Were...

If I were an elephant I'd stomp
With my big feet
And make the noise, rrr!
I'd swing my tail and my trunk.
But for now, I'm happy to be me.

Alicja Wojtkielewicz (6)
Pool House Community Primary School, Ingol

Zebra

If I were a zebra
I'd run and race.
I would eat grass
And run in the pine.
But for now, I'm happy to be me.

Arham Ali (6)

Pool House Community Primary School, Ingol

The Cat

If I were a cat
I would have a tail
And long ears.
I would eat fish and sleep,
But for now, I'm happy to be me.

Esther Uchechukwu Imoh (6)

Pool House Community Primary School, Ingol

Zebra Stripes

If I were a zebra
I'd have black stripes.
I would race
With my friends.
But for now, I'm happy to be me.

Philip Michalkowski (6)
Pool House Community Primary School, Ingol

Rabbit

If I were a rabbit
I'd have brown and fluffy ears.
I would drink water,
But for now, I'm happy to be me.

Lily-May Cookson (5)
Pool House Community Primary School, Ingol

Cat

If I were a cat
I'd have small ears.
I would run away in my garden,
But for now, I'm happy to be me.

Caroline Duncan (6)

Pool House Community Primary School, Ingol

If I Were...

If I were a puppy
I'd lick and hug.
I would be tiny and walk,
But for now, I'm happy to be me.

Alan Kacprowicz (6)
Pool House Community Primary School, Ingol

Cat

If I were a cat
I'd climb fences
And scratch.
I'd eat all the cat food
And play all day.

Kayden Lee Scott (6)
Pool House Community Primary School, Ingol

Cat

If I were a cat I'd run
And sleep
And sniff at cat biscuits
And scratch the sofa.

Kacey May Pickup (6)

Pool House Community Primary School, Ingol

Young Writers Information

We hope you have enjoyed reading this book – and that you will continue to in the coming years.

If you're a young writer who enjoys reading and creative writing, or the parent of an enthusiastic poet or story writer, do visit our website www.youngwriters.co.uk. Here you will find free competitions, workshops and games, as well as recommended reads, a poetry glossary and our blog.

If you would like to order further copies of this book, or any of our other titles give us a call or visit **www.youngwriters.co.uk**.

**Young Writers, Remus House, Coltsfoot Drive, Peterborough, PE2 9BF
(01733) 890066**

info@youngwriters.co.uk